Heroes
and
Villains

George Ivanoff

HORWITZ
MARTIN
EDUCATION

HORWITZ
MARTIN
EDUCATION

Horwitz Martin Education
A Division of Horwitz Publications Pty Ltd
55 Chandos St
St Leonards NSW 2065
Australia

Horwitz Martin Education
Unit 15, Cressex Enterprise Centre
Lincoln Road
High Wycombe, Bucks HP12 3RL
United Kingdom

Text copyright © Black Dog Books 2000
First published 2000

a black dog book
Designed by Josie Semmler
Cover photograph by John Brash. Digital composition by Josie Semmler.
Illustrations by Peter Foster pp. 3, 5, 6, 11, 12, 19, 21, 37, 38, 51, 52, 53, 67, 68,
70, 79, 82.
Printed and bound in Australia by Hyde Park Press.

National Library of Australia
Cataloguing information
Ivanoff, George, 1968–.
  Heroes and villains

Bibliography.
Includes index.
ISBN 0 7253 1949 6.

1. Heroes - Juvenile fiction. 2. Heroes - Juvenile literature.
3. Good and evil. 4. Characters and characteristics. I. Title.
(Series: Phenomena II).

398.352

Thoth
The Egyptian
god of wisdom,
mathematics and writing.

The publishers would like to thank Suzy Zail for permission to reproduce
the photograph on p. 84. Other images are from the editor's, author's and
designer's collections or are in the public domain. Every effort has been
made to contact original sources, where known, for permissions. If an
infringement has inadvertently occurred, the editor wishes to apologise.
The publisher and the editor would like to thank Garry Chapman and Vicki
Hazell, the educational consultants on this series.

1 2 3 4
00 01 02

Contents

Dedication:

As you're growing up, siblings can alternate between being heroes and villains. Eventually you realise that they are ordinary people just like yourself.

This book is for my brother, Andrew.

Acknowledgments:

Sincere thanks to Andrew Kelly, Robyn Crocker, Pete and Jimi Reilly, Wendy Purcell, Dr H. Gibbons and my Mum-in-law, the Rev Jan St James. Thanks, as always, also go to my wife Kerri and my parents for their continued love and support.

Introduction

W HAT MAKES a hero or a villain?
Does a hero have to have great
strength and intelligence of
superhuman proportions? Does a
villain have to be totally evil?

The Concise Oxford Dictionary defines
a hero/heroine as someone admired for
nobility, courage, and outstanding
achievements, and a villain as a person
guilty of, or capable of, great
wickedness.

In fiction, heroes and villains are
usually clear-cut. The hero is all good,
the villain all bad. In old Wild West
films the good guys would be wearing
white hats, while the bad guys would
have black hats. In *Star Wars*, you know
that Darth Vader is the villain because
he's all in black.

In reality, however, there isn't always
such a clear distinction. People don't just

dress in black and white. There are no invading aliens or superheroes with amazing powers. There are just ordinary people—people with the capacity to do bad things as well as good things.

In the real world there is often a very fine line separating hero from villain. Sometimes, a person can be both, depending on how you look at him or her. In a war, the people on either side would see themselves as the heroes and their enemy as the villains.

Sometimes villains are made out to be heroes and heroes are accused of being villains.

In the end, what makes a hero or a villain is often a matter of opinion. As you read this book, ask yourself what you think makes a hero and what makes a villain.

chapter 1

Myths and superheroes

Imagine...you live in a world where monsters and other evil creatures really do exist. Such a world needs extraordinary heroes...

ELIAS RAN FOR HIS LIFE. Twigs and branches crunched underfoot and autumn leaves were scattered as he raced through the forest. The sound of his own ragged breathing roared in his ears. His legs ached and he desperately wanted to stop, to rest—but he knew he couldn't.

Elias tripped. It was as if the tree root had sprung up out of nowhere and made a grab for his foot. As he lay sprawled among the leaves, he could feel the ground shake with each approaching

footstep. The sound of trees splintering as they were swept aside filled the air around him. Looking up, Elias caught a glimpse, through the branches, of reptilian scales moving toward him.

"They're getting closer," he gasped between breaths. "Got to keep moving."

Within seconds he was back on his feet and running. He didn't have much further to go, but he had to stay ahead of his pursuers. He ran on.

As he was reaching exhaustion, Elias finally came to the end of the forest. This, he knew, would be the hardest part. Running clear of the trees, he was now without cover, dashing across open plain.

He didn't look back, but in his mind's eye he imagined the hunting lizard breaking through the last of the trees— the small, sharp eyes in its huge ugly head, scanning the way ahead and fixing on him.

He tried to block out the image, but from the roar of triumph coming from behind, he knew he had been spotted.

Still he kept running. He could now see his destination—the rocky face of Mt Vishnee. There were caves there. Caves where the hunting lizard would not be able to follow. Caves where he hoped he would find help.

He was almost there now. Only 200 metres to go…150…100…50…

There was a blinding flash of light as the ground beneath him exploded. Elias was thrown off his feet. Head spinning, he looked up from where he had landed. Towering over him was the huge shape of the hunting lizard, its scales glistening in the sunlight. It roared and gnashed its teeth against the bit.

Sitting atop the giant lizard was the Hunting Master, one hand on the reins, the other clutching a lance. Without any hurry, the figure raised its lance and pointed it at Elias.

"Help!" screamed Elias. He didn't know what else to do.

Sparks flew from the lance as a bolt of energy streaked toward him. As Elias closed his eyes, expecting to die, someone grabbed him from behind and whisked him out of harm's way.

Opening his eyes, Elias saw a strangely dressed woman standing in front of the hunting lizard, not a trace of fear on her face. This must be Zarina, thought Elias, the legendary hero of the Plains People.

5

The Hunting Master pointed his lance at her, but as the sparks flew, she raised her shield, deflecting them. The Hunting Master howled with rage.

"Make all the noise you want," she called out, drawing her sword, "for you shall hunt no more."

She crouched down as the lizard slashed at her with its front claws.

Then, springing up, she propelled herself through the air, somersaulting and landing on the creature's back.

The Hunting Master's face was a mix of rage and terror as Zarina raised her sword…

THE END

THERE ARE MANY STORIES where the hero or villain has super powers. In the story you just read, the heroine could move very quickly and jump very high. The villain had a lance that shot energy bolts and was riding a giant lizard. Fictitious heroes and villains like this have been around for a very long time.

Superheroes like Superman, Wonder Woman and Spiderman, and the super villains they fight against, are not just comic book creations. These heroes and villains have their origins in the myths and legends of ancient civilisations.

If you compare modern-day superheroes with ancient mythology, you will find a lot of similarities.

Hercules and Superman

There are similarities between the mythical Greek hero Hercules and the comic book superhero, Superman. Both have extraordinary strength. Superman has battled robots, aliens, monsters and super villains like Brainiac. Hercules battled the lion of Nemea, the wild boar of Erymanthus and even a nine-headed monster called

mythology: a body of myths relating to a particular people.

7

the Hydra. He also tamed the flesh-eating mares of Diomedes.

Even as a baby, Hercules displayed great strength, killing two snakes that were sent to kill him.

Both Superman and Hercules were very smart, often using intelligence as well as strength to defeat an enemy. Battling the Hydra needed more than just strength, because if one of its heads was cut off, two new heads would grow in its place. Also, one of those heads was immortal. So, after cutting off a head, Hercules used fire to burn the wound, stopping new heads from growing. He trapped the immortal head under a rock.

Neither Superman nor Hercules was human. Superman came to Earth from another planet, Krypton, while Hercules was the son of Zeus, ruler of the gods.

Today's fictional superheroes have been influenced by mythological heroes.

According to Greek mythology, Prometheus took fire from Olympus as a gift for humans. Zeus punished Prometheus. He was chained to a rock and an eagle was sent to feed on his liver every day.

The need for stories

In today's world we tell stories of heroes and villains in film, television and books. The stories entertain us and also teach us the difference between right and wrong.

Similarly, in ancient times, stories of heroes and villains were used to entertain and teach. But in ancient times, these stories were often linked with religious and spiritual beliefs. While the Greeks told many stories about the gods on Mt Olympus, they also worshipped them, building temples and providing offerings. To the Australian Aborigines, the Dreamtime stories are an explanation of how life on Earth was created.

Jason and the Argonauts

Setting sail aboard the *Argo*, mythological hero Jason led a whole crew of heroes on a quest for the Golden Fleece. Among the Argonauts were Hercules, a great huntress named Atlanta and Theseus, famous for having killed the Minotaur, a creature that was half-man, half-bull.

Among other deeds, Jason and the Argonauts yoked a team of fierce fire-breathing oxen, fought armoured men who sprouted from dragon's

Ancient myths and legends have been told and retold so many times that there are often different versions of the same story. According to one story Jason had 55 men with him aboard the *Argo*, while another version lists 49 men and one woman.

teeth planted in a field, and freed a man named Phineus from the Harpies, which were large birds with girls' faces and long, sharp talons. Finally, they also had to face the sleepless dragon that guarded the Fleece. Using a magic potion, they were able to put the dragon to sleep and get the Golden Fleece.

Samson and Delilah

Heroes didn't always have good fortune. They often made mistakes.

Samson, the biblical hero of the Israelite people, had superhuman strength. He was a great asset to his people in their battles with their enemies, the Philistines. When Samson fell in love with a woman named Delilah, he told her the secret of his strength—his hair, which had never been cut. This was to be Samson's greatest mistake, for Delilah betrayed him to his Philistine enemies for money.

The Philistines shaved off Samson's hair while he slept. When he woke, he was no longer able to resist them, so they gouged out his eyes and took him prisoner, intending to sacrifice him in their temple. But Samson's hair started to grow back, and before they could sacrifice him, his strength returned. Samson pulled down the pillars that supported the temple, killing himself and the Philistines who were with him.

David and Goliath

Of course, not all mythological heroes had super powers. Some of them were just ordinary people faced with extraordinary circumstances.

One of the most famous confrontations between a hero and villain is the biblical story of David and Goliath. The Israelites and the Philistines were at war. The Philistines' champion, Goliath, challenged the Israelites to put forward a champion of their own for single combat to end the war. Goliath was a giant, 3 metres (10 ft) tall and heavily armoured. None of the Israelite soldiers would go to fight him. A boy named David, who was delivering food to the soldiers, heard the giant's challenge and went out to face him. He wore no armour and his only weapon was a sling.

Despite the difference in size and strength, David killed the giant with

sling:
a strap or string used to project a small missile such as a stone.

11

a stone shot from his sling, which struck
Goliath on the forehead.

Villains and monsters

In ancient mythologies, the villains were
not always human. They were often
monsters or half-human creatures like the
Minotaur, which was half-man half-bull.
It lived in the centre of a huge maze and
every ninth year, seven people were put
into the maze as a sacrifice. In order to
stop this, the hero Theseus went into the
maze and killed the Minotaur.

Sometimes, the gods themselves were
the villains. While the gods of Greek
mythology were often heroic protectors,
they could also cause much trouble for
humans such as war and famine as well
as other personal suffering. The goddess
Hera once put a spell on Hercules
causing him to kill his own children.

Minotaur

Medusa and the Gorgons

In Greek mythology, the Gorgons were
monstrous female creatures with sharp
fangs, impenetrable scales and living
snakes for hair. Anyone who looked at
them would instantly be turned to stone.

Medusa, one of the Gorgons, was killed by the hero Perseus, who cut off her head. By looking at her reflection in his shiny shield, he was able to see her without being turned to stone.

Despite being villainous creatures, Gorgons were often drawn on the shields of Greek soldiers and on temples and graves to keep evil away.

Russian folklore has a similar creature called the Gorgonya. She was a woman with snakes in her hair who knew all languages and could kill with a glance. It was said that any man who could cut off her head would be victorious in every battle he fought.

Were all ancient heroes mythical?

There are many different myths and legends, from the gods of ancient Egypt to the Dreamtime of the Australian Aborigines. But were there real heroes in ancient times?

Many myths have their basis in fact. Sometimes, real heroes have reached legendary status. In addition to their heroic

The Dreamtime is a mythological past during which spirit ancestors travelled the land, giving it its physical form and setting down the rules by which the Australian Aboriginal people live.

actions, storytellers kept adding more
and more, until these real people became
part of the mythology.

Gilgamesh

One of the earliest mythical heroes is
Gilgamesh, featured in Sumerian and
Babylonian poetry. According to the
poems, he was only half-human, being
the son of the goddess Ninsun.

The real Gilgamesh was King of Uruk
in Babylonia (modern-day Iraq).

Stories and myths about Gilgamesh
were written on clay tablets in about 2000
B.C. Before that, the stories would have
been told verbally, passed down from one
generation to the next.

Alexander the Great

Alexander
the Great
was King of
Macedonia,
one of the
Greek
states.

Alexander the Great lived from 356 B.C. to
323 B.C. He was a skillful military leader
who led his army to many victories.
Alexander united the Greek states and
conquered many other lands including
Asia Minor, Persia, Egypt and India.

Alexander also founded the city of
Alexandria, which became a world centre
of commerce and learning.

Alexander believed that he was descended from the legendary Greek heroes Achilles and Hercules. In the lands that he conquered, he demanded that people worship him as a god.

According to legend, Bucephalus, Alexander's favourite horse, was descended from the mares of Diomedes which Hercules tamed.

Charlemagne

Charles the King, our Lord and Sovereign
Full seven years hath sojourned in Spain,
Conquered the land, and won the western
  main,
Now no fortress against him
  doth remain...

So begins *The Song of Roland*, an 11th century epic poem about King Charles the Great— Charlemagne. It was the first fictionalised, written account of Charlemagne, who was a real historical figure.

Charlemagne achieved much in his life, but legends about him increased his heroics to the point where several miracles were attributed to him.

Charlemagne with his conquering army.

15

Charlemagne lived from A.D. 742–814. He united, by conquest, nearly all the Christian lands of western Europe and was proclaimed Holy Roman Emperor by Pope Leo III in A.D. 800. In addition to bringing unity to much of Europe, he also brought education. He sponsored monasteries where ancient books were preserved and copied. He also set up monastic schools throughout his realm. The emphasis on education and culture during Charlemagne's reign came to be known as the Carolingian Renaissance.

Although he practised often, Charlemagne never mastered the art of writing. For official documents, he used a stencil to sign his name.

Arthurian Legend

In British legends, Arthur was the son of King Uther Pendragon. As a baby, he was taken away by the wizard Merlin, who became his teacher and later his adviser. When King Uther died, he had no heir other than the missing Arthur. While people argued over who would get the throne, a large stone block with a sword in it appeared mysteriously in the castle courtyard. The inscription on the

renaissance: a revival of art, literature and learning.

stone read: "He who draws this sword from this stone is the rightful king of Britain." Many tried and failed before the young Arthur succeeded.

After being crowned king, Arthur established the Knights of the Round Table. He and his 150 knights rode out to accomplish heroic deeds. Their most famous adventure was the quest for the Holy Grail. In some Celtic legends, they fought giants, monsters and witches.

There has been much debate as to whether Arthur was an historical figure or not. His reality was defended by the Tudor monarchs of England who claimed to be descended from him. Today, it is generally accepted that there was no King Arthur. The character may, however, have been based on a 6th century war-chief.

King Henry VIII is the most famous Tudor monarch. Originally a Catholic, he founded the Church of England so he could divorce his first wife. Henry had six wives altogether.

Mordred—villain or hero?

The villain to Arthur's hero was his nephew, Mordred. During the Battle of Camlann, at which the Knights of the Round Table were defeated, Mordred killed Arthur.

As with many legends and myths that have been told and retold, each version portrays events and people differently.

In most stories, Mordred is portrayed as the villain. However, in one Scottish version he is the hero, fighting for the Scots against the English, who were trying to invade their land.

Who's who?

So, who is a hero and who is a villain? It's a matter of opinion. Often it depends on whose side you are on. Mordred may have been portrayed as a hero by the Scots because of their conflicts with the English. To the Israelites, David was the hero and Goliath the villain, but to the Philistines it would have been the other way around.

Opposing sides each have their own heroes. This is not just true in war, but anywhere there is conflict or competition.

In the 1970s television series, *The Secrets of Isis*, school teacher Andrea Thomas becomes a superhero when she inherits the powers of the ancient Egyptian goddess, Isis.

chapter 2

Playing to win

Imagine...it's the year 2004 and you're on your way to an event you've spent the last four years training for...

Ella TOOK A DEEP breath and looked out the window. They were so high. The land below looked unreal—like a giant map. After a few minutes her view was obscured as the plane passed over a bank of clouds.

Ella was nervous about flying—she'd never been in a plane before. But she was also excited—excited about seeing Athens and excited about competing.

She remembered watching the 2000 Olympic Games on television. She was so excited each time her country had won an event—especially a swimming event. When they won their first swimming medal, she had jumped off the sofa and run around the house yelling and cheering. Her parents had thought she had gone crazy.

"I'm going to the next Olympic Games," she had announced to them, then and there. "I'm going to swim in the Games and I'm going to win a gold medal."

Despite her parents' scepticism, she had started training the very next week. She had gone to see her swimming coach at school and told him that she wanted to train for the next Olympic Games.

"It'll be a lot of work," he had said. "A lot more work than just training for the school squad." He had paused, seeing the determination in her eyes, and then smiled. "But you are the strongest swimmer on our team in your age group. And if you're prepared to put in the work, I see no reason why you couldn't make it to the next Olympic Games."

Ella had certainly put in the work— training each morning before school and even on the weekends. Now, here she was, sitting on a plane on the way to achieving her dream.

Before she left, the school's headmaster

had referred to her as "the school's sporting hero." There was a special assembly in her honour and she'd been given a new watch as a present from the school community.

She looked down at that watch now. Tick, tick, tick. It was one of those water-proof ones you could wear while swimming. Tick, tick, tick. Just 20 minutes before the plane was due to land.

Ella looked out of the window again. They were lower now, flying through the clouds rather than over them. She grinned as she thought about the upcoming competition. She didn't know whether she would win a medal or not, but she had trained hard and she was going to do her best. Whether or not she won gold didn't really seem to matter anymore. She'd made it to the Olympic Games…and that was the real achievement.

THE END

SPORT HAS BEEN LINKED with heroes ever since the ancient Olympic Games in Greece. In today's world, successful sports people are proclaimed heroes, gaining fame and often fortune as well. People like Michael Jordan and Shaquille O'Neal are known all over the world because of their sporting achievements.

In the story you have just read, Ella was called a hero by her school's headmaster, even though she had yet to compete in the Olympic Games. Even if she doesn't go on to win, all her training and hard work are still heroic—because she challenged herself to achieve a goal.

For some athletes, winning a medal is so important that they take drugs to enhance their performance or break the rules to beat their opponents.

During the 1908 London Games, at a service for Olympic athletes, Bishop Ethelbert Talbot of Central Pennsylvania said: "The most important thing in the Olympic Games is not to win but to take part, just as the most important thing in life is not the triumph but the struggle. The essential thing is not to have conquered but to have fought well."

To many people, however, winning is all that matters, especially if there is money involved. It seems that anyone who wins is called a hero.

The ancient Olympic Games

From 776 B.C., Greece held its Olympic Games every four years. Athletes from all the Greek city-states joined in the Games at Olympia. As there were often wars between the city-states, a truce was called for the duration of the Games.

The first recorded winner at the Olympic Games was a runner named Koroibos. He achieved hero status as did many other athletes in successive Games.

Theagenes of Thasos, a boxer and runner, achieved victories at the 75th and 76th Games in 480 and 476 B.C. After his death, the people of Thasos erected a bronze statue in his honour.

Milo of Kroton won six Olympic wrestling events between 540 and 516 B.C. His heroic deeds, however, extended beyond sport. When Kroton was attacked by a neighbouring town, Milo led his people into battle and won. He once saved the life of his friend Pythagoras, a famous philosopher. Pythagoras and his followers were having a meeting in a hall. When the roof began to collapse, Milo

Women were forbidden to compete in, or be spectators at, the ancient Olympic Games. The penalty for breaking this rule was death.

stood and supported the central pillar until they escaped, then he too ran out.

There were villains in ancient times as well. Those caught cheating in the Olympic Games were fined and the money used to make bronze statues of Zeus. These statues were engraved with the offence, then placed on the road to the stadium as a warning to others. The earliest recorded cheater was Eupolus of Thessaly, who bribed boxers in the 98th Games.

The modern Olympic Games

French Baron Pierre de Coubertin was inspired by the ancient Olympic Games to set up a modern equivalent, where athletes from all over the world would come to compete. An International Olympic Committee was formed in 1894 and the very first modern Olympic Games were held in 1896 in the city of Athens in Greece. The first Winter Olympic Games were held in 1924 in the French city of Chamonix.

Women were not allowed to compete in the first modern Olympic Games. Although some women did compete in the 1904 St Louis and 1908 London Games, they were not formally admitted to the Olympic Games until 1912 in Stockholm.

With its motto of *Citius, Altius, Fortius* (Faster, Higher, Stronger), the Olympic Games have encouraged the creation of sporting heroes—people who are the best in their chosen sport.

Jesse Owens

American athlete Jesse Owens became an Olympic hero at the 1936 Berlin Games, winning four gold medals in the 100-metre race (tying the world record), the long jump (setting a new Olympic record), the 200-metre race (setting a new Olympic record) and the 100-metre relay (setting new Olympic and world records). While Jesse was a hero to most of the world, Adolf Hitler saw him as a villain.

Hitler's Olympics were the most spectacular since the modern Games had begun. It was an exercise in propaganda to convince the world of German superiority.

Hitler, Germany's leader, publicly declared the Aryan people as a superior race, and he was confident that the Olympic Games would prove this. Owens, an African American, made a mockery of Hitler's theories by beating Germany's athletes.

Not all Germans agreed with Hitler's views. Luz Long, the German athlete who came second in the long jump, was the first to congratulate Owens on his win.

The best of the best

Australian swimmer, Sarah Durack, achieved hero status when she became the country's first female gold medallist, winning the 100-metre freestyle swimming at the 1912 Stockholm Games. During her swimming career, 1906–1921, Durack broke 11 world records.

Nadia Comaneci is a Romanian gymnast who, at the age of 14, won three gold medals, one silver and one bronze at the 1976 Montreal Games. She was the first woman to score a perfect ten on the parallel bars. She became an immediate hero and appeared on the covers of *Time*, *Newsweek* and *Sports Illustrated* all in the same week. At the 1980 Moscow Games, she went on to win another two gold and two silver medals.

At the 1984 Los Angeles Games, an American runner named Carl Lewis matched Jesse Owens's wins . He went on to win gold medals at the 1988 Seoul Games and the 1992 Barcelona Games.

The Olympic torch is lit in Olympia and carried by relay to the host city where it is used to light the Olympic flame.

Taking the oath

At the opening ceremony of each Olympic Games, one athlete is chosen to represent all the competitors, taking an oath on their behalf:

"In the name of all the competitors I promise that we shall take part in these Olympic Games, respecting and abiding by the rules which govern them, in the true spirit of sportsmanship, for the glory of sport and the honour of our teams."

Unfortunately, not all athletes respect the oath. Cheating and violence have sometimes found their way into the Olympic Games.

Ben Johnson—from hero to villain

At the Seoul Olympic Games in 1988, Canadian sprinter Ben Johnson became a sporting hero for winning gold in the 100-metre run and setting a new world record of 9.79 seconds. His hero status, however, was short-lived. Soon after the race it was discovered that he had been taking anabolic steroids to enhance his performance. His gold medal was taken away and he received a two-year ban from world competition.

Some athletes are willing to do anything to win,

> Anabolic steroids increase a person's lean muscle mass, giving them an extra competitive edge in sports. These drugs can also cause severe physical problems.

including taking drugs. These drugs could give them the edge over other athletes.

Taking these drugs is cheating, and the Olympic Games organisers do their best to stop it. At each Games, hundreds of athletes are tested for drugs through urine sampling.

During the Olympic Games, tests are carried out on urine samples from all medal winners. Anyone found to have used drugs will be banned from further competition and have his or her medal withdrawn.

Does violence make you a villain?

Violence is not permitted at the Olympic Games—but does violent behaviour necessarily make you a villain? Violence broke out at the 1956 Melbourne Games because of the political situation between Hungary and the Soviet Union.

Hungary was under the rule of the Soviet Union. When Hungarians protested the control of their country in 1956, Soviet troops were sent in to stop what was being called the Hungarian Revolution. At the Olympic Games that year, there was tension between the Soviet and Hungarian athletes.

War in the water

When the Hungarian and Soviet water polo teams came to play against each

other, violence occurred. The Hungarian athletes, angry at what was happening in their homeland, took out their feelings on the Soviet team.

Throughout the match, punches and kicks were exchanged, and referees ordered three Soviet and two Hungarian players out of the water. During the final two minutes a Soviet player head-butted a Hungarian, drawing blood.

The violence spread to the audience, but police prevented a riot. The Soviets left the match before it was over and the Hungarian team were declared winners.

The modern game of polo, like water polo, was first played by the British. But, other than the name and the use of a ball, the two games are not at all alike.

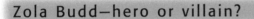

Zola Budd—hero or villain?

As a teenager, South African runner, Zola Budd, became a sporting hero when she set a 500-metre world record of 15 minutes, 1.83 seconds running barefoot. Her home country had been banned from the Olympic Games since 1964 because of its apartheid policies. In order to be able to compete at the 1984 Los Angeles Games, Zola became an English citizen.

In the Games, Zola ran in the 3000-metre race along with the American

apartheid: a system of segregation or discrimination on the basis of race.

favourite, Mary Decker. There was a great deal of publicity before the race as both women were excellent runners.

During the race, Zola accidentally tripped Mary Decker, who fell over. After the race, Decker burst into tears and lashed out at Zola for tripping her and ruining her chance of winning gold. To many people Zola was suddenly a villain. They saw her change of citizenship as cheating and blamed her for Mary Decker not winning the 3000-metres.

Eddie, the Eagle

You don't have to win a medal at the Olympic Games to be a hero. Representing Britain at the 1988 Olympic Winter Games in Calgary, Eddie Edwards finished 55th in a field of 56 ski jumpers—the 56th was disqualified. Eddie became a hero anyway.

Eddie was the first man ever to represent Britain in an Olympic ski jump event. He qualified for the Games because no other British citizen had applied. Although he came last, he was a favourite with the spectators. Eddie kept audiences entertained with his daredevil

Ski jumping is judged on the skier's balance and coordination as well as their jumping technique.

skiing style and quick wit. He was soon dubbed "Eddie the Eagle".

Eddie, a construction worker by trade, was a hero to many because he represented ordinary people. Despite coming 55th, he was trying hard, doing his best and having a good time as well.

"I think what my Olympic participation shows," said Eddie, "is that you don't have to be the best in the world to be popular."

What do you think? Can an athlete be a hero without actually winning?

Bobsledding heroes

An unlikely group of athletes representing Jamaica in the bobsled event, also became heroes at the Calgary Games. Despite antiquated equipment and the lack of snow in Jamaica, these four athletes trained and qualified for the Olympic Games event. They became heroes and an inspiration to other warm-climate countries. Jamaica has competed in the Winter Games again since then and the Virgin Islands entered a bobsled team at the 1994 Lillehammer Games.

The Jamaican bobsled team's participation in the Calgary Games became the inspiration for the film *Cool Runnings*.

It's just not cricket

One of Australia's most acclaimed cricketing heroes is batsman, Sir Donald Bradman. He played in the 1932–1933 season against England—one of the most controversial seasons in cricketing history. In that season, the English team used bodyline tactics—bowling the ball very fast at the body of the batsman, with a group of fieldsmen waiting in a semi-circle on the legside to catch any ball fended off by the batsman. There was little else a batsman could do when faced with this tactic.

During the third test match, Australian Captain Bill Woodfall was struck above the heart. Later in the match, another batsman was struck in the head, resulting in a fractured skull. Police had to be called in to stop Australian spectators from storming the field. To them, the English team had become villains rather than just opponents.

The bodyline tactic was instigated by the English captain, Douglas Jardine. Some of the English fast bowlers objected to the tactic and refused to use it. Relations between England and Australia were very low during this cricket season.

Bodyline tactics have since been outlawed in cricket.

Is bad sportsmanship villainous?

In 1981, Australian cricketing captain and hero Greg Chappell became a villain. In a match against New Zealand, where New Zealand needed five runs from the final ball to win, he ordered his younger brother Trevor to bowl the last ball underarm along the ground. The ball couldn't be hit for six by the New Zealand batter, making sure the team didn't have the chance to score the runs they needed to win. Although it wasn't strictly against the rules, it was considered unsportsman-like behaviour. This tactic was later banned by the cricket authorities.

The winged keel—was it cheating?

In 1851, the New York Yacht Club won a silver trophy, called the One Hundred Guinea Cup, in an English yacht race. Since then, contenders from all over the world have competed for the trophy, now known as the America's Cup.

In 1983, the Australian yacht *Australia II* won. It was the first time in 132 years that the cup was not won by an American team. The captain of *Australia II*, John Bertrand, became a sporting hero to Australians. But he and his team were far from heroes to the Americans. There were accusations of cheating because the *Australia II* had been fitted with a newly designed winged keel. To the Americans, Dennis Conner became the hero when he won the cup back in his yacht *Stars and Stripes* at the next challenge in 1986–1987.

Running with the ball

Sometimes it's the people who break the rules who become heroes. In 1823, a 16-year-old schoolboy named William Webb Ellis picked up the ball during a game of soccer and ran with it. This was against the rules, but his action is said to have been the beginning of the game which came to be known as rugby, named after his school. There is a commemorative stone on the Rugby School grounds with an inscription that reads:

"This stone commemorates the exploit of William Webb Ellis who with a fine disregard for the rules of football, as played in his time, first took the ball in his arms and ran with it, thus originating the distinctive features of the rugby game. A.D. 1823."

Is it a sport?

Sport can sometimes go to extremes. In the World Wrestling Federation (WWF), the competitors wear costumes, have characters and follow a script, with the crowd cheering on their sometimes comical exploits.

The WWF has had heroes with names like Stone Cold Steve Austen, Mankind and The Rock, and villains such as Kane, HHH and The Undertaker.

Interestingly, the heroes and villains often change places over time. Stone Cold Steve Austen began his wrestling career as a villain before progressing to hero status.

Whether the WWF is really a sport or not is debatable. Its main aim is to be entertaining, with spectators cheering for the heroes and booing at the villains.

Not all wrestling is a theatrical performance. At Olympic level it is a serious sport.

Is winning all that counts?

To be a sports hero usually means winning. People like Eddie Edwards are, unfortunately, in the minority—especially in professional sports where large sums of money are at stake. What do you think? Is winning all that counts, or does it take more than that to be a hero?

As a child, Wilma Rudolf had polio. Though unable to walk correctly until she was 11 years old, Wilma became a runner. In the 1960 Rome Olympic Games, she became the first American woman to win three gold medals.

chapter 3
The winner takes it all

Imagine...the year is 1862 and you're in the American Wild West...

NED WATCHED his father come storming into the cabin. He was a large man with a thick brown beard and angry eyes.

"Those Indians are on the war-path," he said, angrily.

He grabbed the rifle from the rack on the far wall and began to check it over. Ned saw the unspoken concern in his mother's eyes. She'd never wanted to come out West in the first place. Life here was hard, and she had often wished that they had stayed in the city.

"This is our land," Ned's father

continued, "and I'll be damned if I let anyone take it from me."

But weren't the Indians here first? thought Ned. Didn't we take the land away from them? It was a thought that had often occurred to him, but one which he had learnt to keep to himself. He was only thirteen and no one took him seriously. If I were an Indian, he mused, I'd be considered almost a man.

He had once brought up the subject and received a cuff across the ears for his trouble. "Damn fool boy," his father had said, "they ain't real civilised people."

They looked like real people to Ned. Sure, their skin was a different colour and they wore funny clothes, but they were still people.

Ned's father suddenly looked up at the sound of approaching horses. With the rifle checked and loaded he headed for the door, cursing as he went.

He never made it out of the cabin. Several arrows came streaking in the moment he opened the door.

THE END

38

NED AND HIS FAMILY are made-up characters, but other elements of this story are true. White settlers in the Wild West did treat the land as their own even though they took it away from the Native Americans. In 1862, the Sioux Indians in the frontier state of Minnesota, did try to take their land back. They attacked the farms of settlers and killed over 450 people before being defeated.

The images of the Wild West presented in films and books are often far from this reality. The Indians are the savage villains and the cowboys are the heroes protecting their homes and their land. Wild West marshals patrol the small town streets saving townsfolk, not only from Indians, but also from outlaws such as Billy the Kid and Jesse James.

How much of this image is real?

The Native Americans

The Native American tribes were living in America long before white settlers arrived. They were not a united people. There were over five hundred different tribes, who spoke many different

Wild West legend Buffalo Bill was a famous pony express rider. He was also known for killing 4280 buffalo in just eight months to feed railroad workers.

languages and hundreds of dialects. They ranged from the Plains tribes such as the Sioux and the Comanches, who hunted buffalo, to the Mandan and Pawnees who farmed pumpkins, beans, squash and corn. The Paiutes and the Gosiutes in the Great Basin region gathered seeds, berries and roots, and hunted rabbits and reptiles.

dialect:

a variation on a language, spoken by people in a particular area or social group.

These varying tribes did not always live together peacefully. In fact, for many tribes, battle was an important part of their culture. War would often be caused by a dispute over who hunted on what land. Land was also important in Native American culture. Individuals did not own land—rather, a tribe used large areas of land communally. The white settlers' idea of owning pieces of land was a foreign concept to them.

The white settlers

As white settlers arrived, the Native Americans were pushed further and further west. Eventually, after being stripped of all their land, they were forced onto small reservations, in areas not used by white settlers.

The white settlers pushing west were farmers, traders and people in search of gold. As far as they were concerned the United States treaties with the Native Americans gave them the right to be there and to claim the land as their own.

Cowboys were often depicted as heroes who protected new settlers from the native dwellers who were known as "savage redskins".

The government

The United States Government intended to treat the Native Americans fairly. George Washington, the first president of the USA, wrote that the "basis of our proceedings with the Indian nations has been, and shall be justice."

Good intentions, however, were not enough. In practice the government was anything but fair. The Native Americans were forced into treaties, which time and again the government would break.

Treaties, treaties and more treaties

In 1778, the first of 370 treaties between the USA and the Native American tribes was signed with the Delaware tribe, whose land had extended from Ohio to the Atlantic. In return for helping the USA against the British during the American War of Independence, the treaty promised the organisation of an Indian state with the Delaware tribe as its head. But, the United States Government didn't kept its side of the treaty. Through 18 further treaties the Delawares were moved to Indiana, then Missouri, Kansas and finally, Oklahoma.

treaty:

a formal agreement between two or more parties.

The last treaty was signed on 12 August 1868 with the Nez Percés. They were guaranteed land in the Wallowa Valley. But the treaty was broken by the USA when gold was discovered in the area.

In 1871, the USA declared that it no longer considered the Native American tribes as separate nations, and therefore no more treaties would be signed. By this time, the Native Americans, who once roamed all the land in America, had only 200,000 sq miles (33,333 sq km), with the white settlers owning 3,000,000 sq miles (5,000,000 sq km).

Plains Indians lived in buffalo-skin tents called tipis. They are portable, easily erected and waterproof. Even with a fire burning inside, a tipi is well ventilated by wind-deflecting smoke flaps.

To the Native Americans, the white man's government was the villain, forcing them off their land. To the settlers, the government was heroic in its actions to secure more land for them.

Custer's last stand

General Custer is often portrayed as a great hero of the Wild West whose career came to an end when he and his men were ambushed by Indians at the Battle of Little Big Horn. But the truth is a far cry from the legend.

Custer graduated from West Point at the bottom of his class and with a huge number of demerit points. He was given the rank of General through a battlefield commission during the Civil War. His success in the war was a result of his reckless methods and wild charges, which resulted in the highest casualty numbers of any commander.

In 1867, Custer's rank was suspended for a year because he abandoned his command to visit his wife. He himself, had ordered that other deserters be shot without a hearing.

In 1868, he took part in a military campaign against the Plains tribes, who had been resisting the white man's authority. Discovering a large camp of Native Americans along the banks of the

Horses were very important to the Plains Indians who used them for hunting as well as in battle. The horses were often decorated with head-dresses.

43

Little Big Horn River, Custer ignored his scout's report on the size of the camp and decided to attack without waiting for reinforcements. He divided his forces to attack from two different directions and so was undermanned in both places.

Sioux warrior's song to his horse.
My horse be swift in flight
Even like a bird;
My horse be swift in fight.
Bear me now to safety
Far from the enemy's arrows,
And you shall be rewarded
With streamers and ribbons red.

The attack was a surprise to the Native Americans, who certainly didn't plan an ambush. Their leader, Chief Crazy Horse, was an experienced warrior and brilliant tactician. He planned a successful defence during which Custer was killed.

Despite Custer's mistake in attacking, he was treated as a hero and given a hero's burial at West Point. For many years, Native American accounts of the battle were simply not believed by the white inhabitants.

The cowboys

The term "cowboy" came into general use after the American Civil War. It referred to anyone who tended cattle in the West, but was most associated with those who moved cattle great distances across the country from where they were bred and grazed to where they were sold.

> **tactician:** someone who plans the movement of troops during a battle.

The heroic image of the cowboy, six-shooter blazing, fighting off Indians and wild animals, is not a very realistic one. While some cowboys did actually shoot it out with Native Americans, or break-in wild horses or lasso bears, it was not something that happened often.

A cowboy's life was mostly just hard and boring. Taking cattle from one part of the country to another often took many weeks. Day after day it was the same routine. Keep the cows together and keep them moving.

Cowboy George Duffield kept a diary when he drove a herd of cattle from Texas to Iowa in 1866. He mentions losing belongings while crossing a river, not eating for more than 60 hours, having to rescue cattle that were stuck in mud after a storm, and sickness among his men. Not a very glamorous or heroic lifestyle.

Not all cowboys were white. Many of them were Mexican or African American.

Outlaws and lawmen

Cowboys rarely had gunfights. Most gunfights happened among gamblers and professional criminals, and the lawmen who tracked them down.

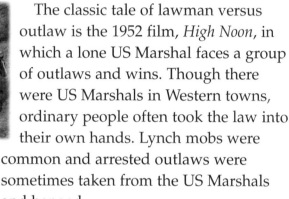

The classic tale of lawman versus outlaw is the 1952 film, *High Noon*, in which a lone US Marshal faces a group of outlaws and wins. Though there were US Marshals in Western towns, ordinary people often took the law into their own hands. Lynch mobs were common and arrested outlaws were sometimes taken from the US Marshals and hanged.

The Texas Rangers were unique lawmen who wore neither badges nor uniforms. They patrolled vast areas of barren land and had a reputation for always catching the criminals they were pursuing.

Wild West fiction

During the 1800s, Wild West stories were very popular with people in the big eastern cities. Cheaply produced novels were filled with Indian villains, gunfights, outlaws and cowboy heroes. Sometimes, they portrayed outlaw killers such as Jesse James as swashbuckling heroes. This created an unrealistic image of the West.

In reality, gunfights rarely happened like they did in fiction. Just after the Civil War, cowboy George Littlefield got into an argument with a neighbour. They each pulled a gun and squeezed the triggers. Both guns misfired. The neighbour ran behind a tree before Littlefield finally shot him. There was no hero or villain here, just two people who got into a fight.

Civil wars

England erupted into civil war in 1642 with Parliament against King. The parliamentary forces won and Charles I was arrested, tried and executed in 1649. It was he who was seen as the villain and Oliver Cromwell, the most prominent of the parliamentary leaders, was the hero.

After Cromwell's death in 1658, the tables were turned again and the army revolted to bring back the monarchy. Cromwell was now the villain, and the new king, Charles II, was the hero.

The American Civil War began in 1861, when the southern Confederate states claimed independence from the rest of the USA. One of the main problems was the issue of slavery. The United States Government was finally outlawing slavery. The southern states depended on

During his trial, King Charles I refused any defence. He believed in his divine right to rule and was certain that he would be found innocent.

slave labour for running their huge cotton plantations and wanted to retain it. Civil war broke out. The North eventually won and slavery was abolished.

Hero of the Philippines

Returning to the Philippines in 1983 after a three-year exile, political activist

Benigno Aquino was assassinated. After his death, Aquino's wife, Corazon, carried on the political struggle against the regime of Ferdinand Marcos.

Marcos had been democratically elected as president in 1965. But, in 1972, after a period of civil unrest, Marcos declared martial law. From then on, he ruled as a dictator, using the military to stay in power.

Corazon ran against Marcos in the 1986 presidential election. Marcos declared himself winner but was accused of rigging the election. This stirred up a great deal of unrest and Corazon led a non-violent people's power campaign which overthrew Marcos.

Corazon Aquino became the first female president of the Philippines.

Slave labour has been used by many cultures through the ages. The pyramids of Egypt were built by slaves about four thousand, five hundred years ago.

She is a hero to her people for bringing Marcos's tyranny to an end. Had she lost, however, Marcos would undoubtedly have portrayed her as the villain.

Who's the hero and who's the villain?

Sometimes it is difficult to tell who is the hero and who is the villain. In 1789, the crew of the HMS *Bounty*, led by first mate Fletcher Christian, mutinied against their captain, William Bligh. Bligh and the 18 men who remained loyal to him were cast adrift in a small boat. The men who mutinied saw Bligh as the villain, turning against him because of his harsh treatment. But, what they did was against the law, so they were seen as the villains.

Bligh went on to become the Governor of New South Wales and again faced rebellion among his men. The officers had, over the years, established a trade monopoly in which rum was their main product. Bligh's attempt to break this monopoly resulted in the Rum Rebellion (1808–1810) during which he was deposed by his soldiers and imprisoned.

monopoly: one group of people having complete control in the trade of particular goods or services.

Despite his failures, Bligh was an accomplished marine surveyor and naval officer. In 1811, he was promoted to admiral. But was he a hero or a villain?

What if things were different?

What if England had won the war against the United States? What if Corazon Aquino had failed and Marcos remained in power? What if Germany had won the Second World War? What if the Native Americans had been able the drive the white settlers out of their country?

Many new settlers travelled across America to the West in wagon trains. Each family had its own covered wagon.

Things would have been very different. Think about it, there would have been a completely different set of heroes and villains.

chapter 4

Fighting the system

Imagine...you live in a time and place ruled by a ruthless and unjust king who mistreats his people...What will you do?

P EOPLE RAN from the streets of the tiny village as they saw the horses approaching. In a cloud of dust, twelve men came riding into the town. As they watched from the doors and windows of their homes, the riders came down along the deserted street into the village square at the centre.

I watched from the door of my father's bakery, as the three village leaders came out to meet the Sheriff and his men.

"Welcome to our village, Sheriff Morgan," said William, one of the leaders. Of course, no one in the village really welcomed a visit from the Sheriff and his men.

Morgan came down off his horse and produced a rolled up parchment from his tunic. He was a tall, grim-looking man, with thin cruel lips and a heavy brow that almost hooded his eyes. He untied the ribbon that held the scroll and unrolled the parchment. Clearing his throat noisily, he began to read.

"The King decrees that, effective immediately, taxes shall be doubled. Any man who refuses to pay, shall be arrested and imprisoned for a period of two years, during which time he shall have the honour of working in the King's mines."

The Sheriff rolled the parchment up and tucked it away in his tunic. He turned to the three men before him.

"It shall be your responsibility to collect the taxes from your village and have them waiting for me. I shall return in three days time for the first payments."

The three leaders stared at each other, disbelief plain on their faces. The Sheriff then returned to his horse, ready to mount.

"But we can't," William protested.

Morgan whirled around to face them again, eyes blazing, daring the three of them to say something more.

"What?"

Each of the other two men put a restraining hand on William's shoulders and shook their heads. William shrugged them off and stepped forward.

"We can't pay the new taxes," he said. "We barely have enough to pay the old ones."

Morgan smiled for the first time. "Are you refusing to pay the tax?"

"I'm saying that we physically cannot pay it."

Morgan turned to his men. "Arrest that man in the name of the King for refusing to pay his taxes."

Two men swiftly dismounted and grabbed William. When William began to struggle one of the men struck him on the back of the head with a club. They then dragged his unconscious body and slung it onto the back of one of the horses.

"Anyone else refusing to pay the lawful taxes?" asked the Sheriff.

In the silence that followed he strode back to his horse and mounted it.

As the Sheriff and his men left the village, I decided I had to do something. Not here, not now, but some day soon. I was certain that what the Sheriff and the King were doing was not fair. Someone had to stand up to them—to fight for what was right. And that someone was going to be me.

THE END

THERE IS A story tradition of fighting against the unjust system. Tales such as Robin Hood and Zorro are about fighting for what's right and protecting the common people. The story you have just read portrays an unfair system, where the ordinary people are being unfairly treated by those in authority. In this sort of situation, people who stand up and fight against the system often become heroes—at least to the people they are fighting for.

Zorro first appeared in *The Curse of Capistrano* by Johnston McCulley in 1919. Set in early 19th century California it tells the story of a rich land owner, Don Diego de la Vega, who at night became Zorro (Spanish for fox), fighting evil and defending the weak and oppressed.

Folk heroes such as Robin Hood appear in popular stories and legends which are passed down through the generations. Robin Hood was a hero to the ordinary people of England, but to the Sheriff of Nottingham, he was the villain.

Robin Hood, as we know the character today, was a nobleman who took to the forest as an outcast. He helped the English peasants who were being oppressed by the Sheriff of Nottingham and Prince John, while King Richard was off fighting in the crusades. He stole from the rich to give to the poor. He was struggling against a system where the peasants were being over-taxed and mistreated.

Changing over time

The stories of Robin Hood, or Robyn Hode as he was known earlier, are fiction. They were first told in the form of ballads by travelling minstrels. One of the first printed stories of Robin's adventures dates from 1489. *A Lytell Jeste of Robyn Hode* was a poem written by a man named Wynken de Worde.

In the early medieval ballads there was no mention of Maid Marion, Prince John or King Richard. The king in these early stories was Edward and Robin was not a nobleman, but a yeoman. During the 16th century the tales turned Robin into an earl whose lands were taken away. King Richard and Maid Marian were introduced into the stories at this time.

The tradition of change has carried on to modern times, as film and television have further adapted the story. The television series, *Robin of Sherwood*, had Robin and his men battling evil sorcerers

yeoman:
a servant in a noble or royal household.

and witches as well as the Sheriff of Nottingham.

Despite the changes to the legend over time, the theme of Robin heroically helping the peasants has remained.

Maid Marion as hero

King Richard I of England was known as the Lion Heart because of his bravery in the Crusades.

Maid Marian was introduced into the Robin Hood legend in the 16th century. Her character has since progressed from a simple love-interest to a hero in her own right. In more recent adaptations, she was fighting right alongside Robin. She was even elevated to the leading part in the television series *Maid Marian and Her Merry Men*.

Who were the real heroes and villains of Robin's time?

Although Robin Hood is a fictitious character, the stories as they have developed have included some real historical figures. King Richard the Lion Heart really was King of England from 1189 to 1199. Prince John really was Richard's brother, and he went on to rule England after his brother's death. John was King from 1199 to 1216.

The Robin Hood stories portray Richard as the valiant hero–king, off fighting in the Crusades, while his cowardly, villainous brother plots to steal his throne. This is not a realistic portrayal of events. Richard may have been an heroic military leader and a good warrior, but he wasn't a very good king.

During his time as king he was only in the country he ruled for two short periods—one of three months, the other of two months. The rest of the time he was off waging war in France, Sicily and Palestine. Richard's constant wars cost a great deal of money and put financial strain on the country.

King Richard went to battle in a full suit of chainmail with this helmet to protect his face.

After Richard's death, John was left in charge of a country that was having internal upheavals as well as facing attacks from outside. He did his best to return stability to England, but in 1215, King John was forced by rebellious nobles to concede a list of privileges to the nobility and to the Church. This list is known as the Magna Carta and is held to be "the cornerstone of English liberties."

Do you think the Robin Hood stories portray these two kings fairly? Was either one a hero or a villain?

Real people in fictional stories

Many other fictional stories have included real historical figures who have not always been accurately portrayed. Alexander Dumas's novel, *The Three Musketeers*, is one such story. Although D'Artagnan, Athos, Porthos and Aramis were fictional characters, Cardinal Richelieu and King Louis XIII were real. In the book, Richelieu was a scheming villain, but was he in real life? Richelieu did indeed amass great power. Being on Louis XIII's royal council, he had much control over policy decisions. There was also opposition to his power. But neither his power nor the opposition to it were as great as in the book. In real life, Richelieu was more a politician than a villain.

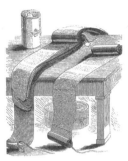

The Magna Carta was written on rolls of parchment. Clause 45 states: "We will appoint as justices, constables, sheriffs or bailiffs only such as know the law of the realm and mean to observe it well."

Fighting for freedom

In the real world there have been many heroic revolutionary figures who have fought for what they believed to be right. Some of these people have already been mentioned in the last chapter. The Native American warrior chief, Crazy Horse, may have been seen as a villain by white settlers for his defeat of General Custer,

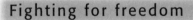

but to his fellow Indians he was a hero, striking a blow for their freedom. Benigno Aquino and his wife, Corazon, were seen as villains by Ferdinand Marcos, but to the Philippino people, they were heroes, struggling against an unfair system.

The French Revolution

The French Revolution was begun in 1789 by people who were struggling against the reign of King Louis XVI. The revolution succeeded, but the new government eventually created a system which was worse than that of the King.

Beginning in September 1793, the Reign of Terror saw the new government executing hundreds of people who were considered to be potential enemies. In the last six weeks of the Terror, nearly 1400 people were sent to the guillotine which was nicknamed, Madame Guillotine.

This period in history gave rise to a famous fictional hero, the Scarlet Pimpernel. An English nobleman, he travelled to France to save the lives of people who were about to be sent to the guillotine.

The Statue of Liberty was a gift from France to commemorate the centennial of USA independence.

guillotine:

an instrument of execution which beheaded people with a large, heavy blade.

Fight for equality

Perhaps one of the longest struggles in history has been the struggle for equality. It is the struggle to change a system that is unfair to a part of its population, denying one group the privileges it gives to another. The struggle for racial equality in America and in South Africa has seen many heroes. The struggle of women to be treated equally with men has also seen many heroes.

segregation: keeping people of different races apart.

Civil rights in America

As late as the 1950s, segregation between backs and whites was still legal in America. Separate drinking fountains and separated seating areas in movie theatres still existed. African Americans were required by law to give up bus seats to white Americans. But there was a growing civil rights movement, demanding equality for black and white.

On 1 December 1955, an African-American woman named Rosa Parks became a hero to the civil rights

Mahatma Gandhi led a non-violent movement to free India from British rule. After many years of struggle and imprisonment, he finally succeeded in negotiating independence for India in 1947.

movement when she refused to give up her bus seat to a white person. She was arrested for her defiance of the law.

African-American singer Josephine Baker was also well known as a civil rights activist. She refused to perform in a venue that segregated its audience. Because of her actions, audiences were first integrated in Las Vegas nightclubs. Josephine was also a Second World War hero, working as an undercover spy for the French Resistance. She died in 1975 and was buried in Paris. She was the first American woman to be buried in France with military honours.

Martin Luther, a leader of the 16th century Reformation, fought against the established laws of the day. Martin Luther King Jnr, like his namesake, fought for reform on the basis of moral principles.

Dr Martin Luther King Jnr

"I have a dream that my four children will one day live in a nation where they will not be judged by the colour of their skin but by the content of their character."

It is for these words that Dr Martin Luther King Jnr is most remembered. One of the best known American civil rights activists, King became a hero to people all over the world through his fight for racial equality. King urged for organised, non-violent mass action (protests, rallies and marches) to bring attention to the cause of African Americans. "We must not allow our creative protests to degenerate into physical violence," he said.

Thanks largely to the efforts of King, and other activists like him, United States President, L. B. Johnson, finally signed the Civil Rights Act in 1964. That year, King was awarded the Nobel Peace Prize.

Apartheid in South Africa

A difficult struggle for civil rights also existed in South Africa, where the government's apartheid policies led to much violence and hatred. The African National Congress was an organisation that fought for equal rights. One of its leaders and heroes was Nelson Mandela. He struggled for many years against the injustices of the apartheid policies. He was arrested in November 1962 and imprisoned. Throughout his time in prison he proved to be an inspiration to other civil rights activists.

The world lost a hero when Martin Luther King Jnr was assassinated in 1968.

In 1989, Willem F. De Klerk became president and immediately began a process for dismantling apartheid. In 1990, he lifted a 30-year ban on the

African National Congress and other black-liberation parties and had Nelson Mandela released from prison. De Klerk and Mandela then worked together for the complete removal of apartheid.

In 1993, Nelson Mandela and Willem F. De Klerk were the joint recipients of the Nobel Peace Prize.

Black people were allowed to vote for the first time in the 1994 elections, and Nelson Mandela was elected President of South Africa. De Klerk's National Party formed a coalition government with the African National Congress, with De Klerk acting as Mandela's deputy-president.

The women's movement

Women have also had a long struggle to be treated equally with men. Women were not given the same opportunities for education and work as they were expected to get married, have children and look after a family. When they did work, women were paid less for doing the same work as men. They were also denied the right to vote.

In 1872, American women's rights activist Susan B. Anthony was arrested for illegally voting in that year's presidential election. She was one of the heroes of the women's suffrage movement. She and Elizabeth Cady Stanton co-founded the National Woman Suffrage Association in America.

> Australia was ahead of England and America in women's suffrage, with South Australia leading the way and first allowing women to vote in 1894.

Susan B. Anthony drafted an amendment to the constitution to give women the right to vote. The amendment was first proposed in 1878 and finally accepted in 1920.

Is fighting the system always heroic?

Sometimes, fighting the system is not heroic, no matter what the people who are fighting may think.

Computer hackers often see themselves as heroically fighting the system. What they're really doing is breaking the law and causing a lot of harm.

Individuals have often fought the system when they believe it to be corrupt, even though they make themselves outcasts in the process. However, what they believe to be right is not necessarily so—it's just their way of looking at the situation.

> **suffrage:**
> the right to vote in political elections.

Being a hero is also a matter of perception or how you look at a situation. To a group of villains, another villain may be a hero. A computer hacker may be a hero to other hackers, though he or she is regarded as a villain by most people.

In the film *War Games*, a teenager hacks into the USA's defence computer and almost causes World War III.

chapter 5

Heroic villains

Imagine...the year is 1739 and you are on the outskirts of the town of Belper in England...

RICHARD PEERED out from his hiding place in the dense shrubbery. In the distance, he could see the carriage approaching. He ducked quickly when he saw his father on the other side of the track.

Richard could feel his heart beating faster. He was excited because he had never seen a robbery before. But he wasn't supposed to be here, so he was scared his father might see him. Time and again his father had said it was too dangerous for him to come along. But

Richard couldn't understand this. There was no danger in the stories his father told him.

Richard's father was the infamous highwayman, Jack Robertson. He would hide by the side of a road and wait for a passing carriage. When a suitable one came along, he would ambush it and rob the people on board. There was always plenty of money, because his father only robbed rich travellers. And there was never any trouble because travellers were too scared of highwaymen to resist. That's what his father always told him. To Richard, his father was a hero, looking after him and his mother.

As the sound of the carriage wheels grew louder, Richard wanted to take another look, but he couldn't risk being seen by his father. Suddenly, Richard heard a gunshot. The sound was so loud, he almost jumped out from his hiding place. Richard had never heard a gunshot before—it was frightening. But why had a gun been fired, he wondered.

Calming down, he decided he could chance a look. As he peered over the shrubbery, he saw his father, pistol in hand, yelling at the carriage driver.

"If you value your life, you'll sit up there without moving."

The carriage driver nodded, and Jack Robertson strode over to the carriage door, yanking it open.

"Your money or your life!" he demanded, levelling the pistol at the people inside.

Richard heard a woman scream and a man's pleading voice saying, "We've got hardly any money."

"I'll take what you've got," said Jack, waving the pistol menacingly. "And the pocket watch and those rings you're wearing."

"But they're our wedding rings," the woman protested.

"In the bag," he shouted, throwing a small sack into the carriage, his pistol still pointed at the passengers.

This isn't how it's supposed to happen, thought Richard. Dad said he only ever robbed rich people who could afford to spare some money for the likes of us. It doesn't sound like these people are rich. And why is Dad taking their wedding rings? This isn't right.

Richard was roused from his thoughts

by more shouting. He looked up to see his father make an angry grab for something inside the carriage. While Jack was preoccupied, Richard saw the carriage driver climb down to the road. He had something in his hand—it looked like a small club. He started to move toward Richard's father.

Richard was about to yell out a warning when his father whirled around, saw the carriage driver and levelled his pistol. Richard couldn't believe his eyes. His father had always said that there was no killing involved.

"No-o-o!" screamed Richard, but his voice was drowned out by the sound of the pistol firing...

THE END

FIGHTING AGAINST an unjust system has often meant going outside the law— and these outlaws have often become heroes. But what about people breaking the law for their own personal gain? Could a criminal be considered a hero?

There is a tendency to romanticise criminals—to lessen the severity of their actions and make them seem heroic. There is nothing heroic about stealing or murdering people. But sometimes, criminals do more than just commit crimes.

Your money or your life?

English highwaymen were robbers and killers. They didn't just rob from the rich, they stole from anyone they came across.

In the story you have just read, Richard has a heroic vision of his father. Similarly, many people have had, and still do have, a heroic vision of real highwaymen, especially Dick Turpin.

Dick Turpin

In fiction, Dick Turpin has been presented as a swashbuckling hero, someone who only robbed from the rich. In the 1980s there was even a television series presenting Turpin as a humorous hero. In real life he was very different.

Born in 1705, Turpin was a butcher who began stealing cattle after falling on hard times. Soon after, he joined the Gregory Gang and began housebreaking.

When a number of the gang were arrested, Turpin teamed up with another criminal, Robert King. They took to the coaching routes, robbing travellers.

While escaping arrest, Turpin accidentally shot and killed Robert King's brother. Hiding in the forest, Turpin was tracked down by a woodsman named Thomas Morris. Turpin murdered him to avoid capture.

Highwaymen were often depicted as dashing and fearless, but they were simply thieves and murderers.

To escape the law, Turpin assumed a false name, John Palmer, and set up a legal business in horses and cattle. In 1739, he was arrested for shooting a cockerel. While under arrest, his true identity was discovered. Turpin was hanged on 7 April 1739. He was buried in St George's Churchyard in Fishergate, York. The inscription on his headstone was: "R.T. 33."

cockerel: a young male chicken.

Villain in armour

Few criminals have captured the public's imagination as much as Australia's famous bushranger, Edward 'Ned' Kelly.

Kelly, already a horse-thief, joined up with his brother Dan and two other men on the border of New South Wales and Victoria. The Kelly Gang, as they became known, committed a series of daring robberies from 1879 to 1880.

In June 1880, they were trapped by police in the town of Glenrowan. During the shoot-out with police, Kelly was wounded and the other gang members killed. Later that year, Kelly was taken to the Melbourne Gaol, where he was hung.

It was a difficult time and there was a great division between poor working-class people and rich landowners. So, Ned Kelly became a hero to many workers, who saw him as struggling against the same rich landowners as themselves.

Since his death, Kelly's popularity has continued to grow. These days Ned has almost become a national icon, with his portrait appearing on

Ned Kelly wore home-made armour when committing his crimes. His unusually shaped helmet has now become famous.

everything from famous paintings to tourist souvenirs.

Despite all the hero-worship, Kelly was a criminal—just one of many bushrangers who terrorised the Australian countryside in the late 1800s. Can someone who robbed and murdered be a hero?

Villains at sea

Pirates, active in the 16th and 17th centuries, were criminals. They took over other ships, often by force, robbed them and sometimes killed the crew. Yet pirates have become romanticised and heroic in much fiction. Why?

Although pirates were brutal criminals, it needs to be remembered that they lived in brutal times. To many people, piracy offered benefits that no other life could. In a time of kings and tyranny, pirates had quite democratic practices. A pirate crew would elect their own captain and they voted on most decisions, such as where to sail to or whether to attack another ship. Stolen goods were divided fairly between a crew. Pirates also had a form

When pirate ships fought under the Jolly Roger flag, which was black with a white skull and crossed bones, it meant that they would show mercy to the crew of the other ship.

of disability insurance. If a pirate lost an arm or leg in battle they were paid compensation. If they were killed, their families sometimes received payments.

In a time when slavery was common, piracy offered black slaves a chance at freedom, where they had the same rights as white pirates. In fact, up to a third of many pirate crews were black. Even women were sometimes able to become pirates, with both Anne Bonny and Mary Reed becoming quite famous for their exploits.

Pirates also tended to treat their prisoners well. Although crews that resisted were usually slaughtered, those who surrendered were often spared. They were even well treated in the hopes of encouraging other crews to surrender. The infamous pirate captain, Blackbeard, once even convinced his crew to spare the life of a merchant that they hated.

Some pirate ships even had rules such as no smoking below decks after sunset, lights out at 8 p.m. and no gambling. So, although pirates were breaking the law, there is some basis for why they have

In the early 1800s, Mrs Ching, a famous Chinese pirate, assumed command of an entire pirate fleet when her husband was killed.

sometimes been portrayed in a favourable light.

What do you think? Do their democratic ways make up for their criminal actions?

The roaring twenties

Organised crime was a big problem in America in the 1920s. Large organisations conducted illegal business all over the country. These gangsters were responsible for many deaths, injuries and robberies, and yet some people saw them as heroes.

Al Capone was a famous gangster in the 1920s. Police were never able to prove his involvement in organised crime. When he was finally sent to gaol in 1931, it was for failing to pay income tax.

In 1920, Prohibition was introduced into America with the 18th amendment to the constitution. Prohibition meant that it was illegal to produce, transport or sell alcohol. The gangsters of the time took advantage of this by starting illegal production and distribution of alcohol.

Illegal saloons, called speakeasies, were established in cities all across the country. Many people in America opposed the prohibition of alcohol, which they saw as unfair. To them, the gangsters who opposed this prohibition became heroes. They were seen as fighting an unjust system, almost like modern-day Robin Hoods.

In reality, however, the gangsters were not fighting the system—they were exploiting it. They didn't want to change the system. They were using the system to illegally make money from it. The trade of illegal alcohol was so profitable that entire criminal empires were formed. Are these gangsters heroes or villains?

Virtual villains

With the advent of computers and the Internet, heroes and villains have crossed over into the virtual world. Films such as *Hackers*, portray teenage hackers as misunderstood misfits who are fighting the system. Cyberpunk fiction often portrays them as heroes. There's a whole sub-culture based around hacking into computers, with experts being idolised and treated as heroes by other hackers. There are web sites, bulletin-boards and e-zines all dedicated to hacking.

Cyberpunk is a style of science fiction which deals with a computerised future where people interact with machines and technology has almost taken over.

Real life hackers illegally break into other people's computers, stealing their information, stealing money from bank accounts, damaging programs and destroying files. These people create and release computer viruses capable of causing billions of dollars worth of damage. These are the actions of a criminal, not a hero.

Breaking the law

Villainous people can sometimes be seen as heroes either because of what they do or because of who they do it to. But whether people see them as heroes or villains, one thing remains certain—they are breaking the law.

chapter 6

Ordinary people

Imagine...you're about to be faced with the one thing in life that you are truly terrified of...
and someone's life depends on you overcoming that fear...

MARK SCREAMED as he fell into the water. He had walked out onto the slippery rocks, showing off and teasing his older sister for being such a scaredy-cat. He had been hopping on one foot when he slipped and fell into the river.

Lyn watched helplessly from the river bank as her brother was swept along with the current.

"Mark," she yelled out, jogging along beside the river, "swim back to the edge."

Having recovered from the surprise of

falling into the water, Mark started to swim across to the river bank. At first it looked like he was going to make it, but the current was quite strong and Mark soon began to tire. He was not far from the edge when the current began to sweep him out toward the centre again.

They were a long way from the camp site, so Lyn knew there was no point in screaming for help. Their parents wouldn't hear them. It was up to her now. But what was she going to do? She shivered as she ran along the bank, watching her brother struggle against the current. She couldn't go into the water— she just couldn't.

Up ahead she spotted another outcrop of rocks.

"Mark," she yelled out again. "Try and make it to those rocks."

As Mark continued to swim, Lyn raced off toward the trees, grabbed the largest branch she could carry and ran back toward the rocks. Stopping just short of them, she looked out across the water. Mark wasn't far off. At the rate he was swimming, he would miss the rocks. She would have to go out on the slippery surface and hold out the branch.

She took a deep breath, trying to calm herself. Then she stepped out onto the rock. Careful not to slip, she made her way to the edge and held out the branch.

"Grab the branch!" she called out.

As the river brought Mark near the rocks, he surged forward and managed to clamp a hand onto the branch. Lyn began to pull him in, relief flooding through her. Mark made it to the edge, but just as he was reaching out toward Lyn, he slipped again. Falling backwards, his head struck the edge of a rock and he was dragged under the water.

There was nothing else for Lyn to do— she had to go into the water. She closed her eyes momentarily as the memories came flooding back.

It was last summer. The final day of the school camp. She and another girl from the swim team were at the beach. They splashed out into the waves. Despite earlier warnings about not swimming out too far, they dared each other to see how far out they could get. They swam out quite a distance. But there was a powerful rip out beyond the breakers. She and Debbie were dragged down. Lyn had screamed and screamed until a lung full of water silenced her and blackness came.

She had woken up on the shore, an ambulance officer looking down at her. "She's back," he had said. As she had sat up, she saw Debbie lying on a stretcher and the ambulance officer had pulled a sheet up over her head.

Lyn shook her head and opened her eyes. She had no choice, either she went into the water, or her brother died. She took a deep breath and dived in.

THE END

LYN CONQUERED her greatest fear by diving into the water to save her brother. Her actions were heroic, not only because she was willing to risk her own life to save his, but also because she was doing it despite her fear. Lyn was just an ordinary girl in every other way.

Heroes and villains are all around us in everyday life. Not heroes like Hercules or Superman, or villains like Medusa or the Hydra, but ordinary people—people whose actions are heroic or villainous because of the circumstances they find themselves in.

Are bullies villains?

You find bullies in everyday life—at school, at work, on the street. These people seem to enjoy making life difficult for others. They pick on those weaker than themselves.

The guy at school who steals your lunch. The person at work who makes fun of you all the time. The kid who lives at the end of your street and tries to beat you up. They are all ordinary people. Do you think they're villains?

Can a job be heroic?

Just as there are villains in everyday life, there are also heroes. Every day, doctors, nurses and ambulance drivers save lives.

Every day, police patrol our streets, trying to make our world a safer place to live in. Every day, firefighters risk their lives to put fires out and save people and their homes. Every day, social workers and volunteers help people in need.

Emergency workers and volunteers use the "Jaws of Life" to cut open crashed cars to free people who are trapped inside them.

Are these people heroes? Are voluntary workers, such as volunteer firefighters, more heroic than those who are paid to do the job? What do you think?

Can a company be a villain?

Does a villain or a hero necessarily need to be a person? Can a company or an organisation be a villain or hero? There are organisations, such as the Salvation Army, the Brotherhood of St Laurence and the Red Cross, that help thousands of people everyday. To many people, these organisations are heroic.

Similarly, can the policies and actions of a company make it a villain? Or is it the people who run the company?

Who was the real villain of the Titanic disaster?

On 15 April 1912, the giant luxury liner *Titanic* struck an iceberg and sank. That night, 1490 people lost their lives.

Over the years, numerous people have been accused of being the villain. Was the captain a villain for sailing the ship too fast in dangerous waters? Was Bruce Ismay, the representative of the company that owned and built the *Titanic*, a villain for encouraging the captain to push the ship to greater speeds? Or maybe the real villains were the people who ran the White Star Line, the company that owned and built the ship?

There were 2207 people aboard the *Titanic*, but there were only enough life boats for 1178 people. The company didn't supply more lifeboats because they cluttered up the decks and, after all, it was claimed the ship was unsinkable.

The accommodation for first class shipping passengers was so grand and luxurious it would have been suitable for a palace.

Villains of the Titanic

There were three classes of passengers aboard the *Titanic*. Of the people who died that night, the majority were in third class. As the ship started to sink, the crew were more concerned with saving the people in first class. Women and children from first class were allowed onto the boats first, then those from second class, then those from third. But there were reports of third class passengers being kept below deck and not being allowed up to where the life boats were.

After the disaster, the United States Congress held an investigation into the events of the sinking. They interviewed dozens of passengers, only three of whom were third class. Two of the three stated that they had been kept from going up to the deck, but the investigation never followed up their claims. Even the newspaper reports were mostly about the first class passengers.

Were the crew members who ignored third class passengers villains? What about the Congress investigators and the newspaper reporters— were they villains? Or, perhaps there weren't really any villains? Maybe it was just the

When the White Star Liner *Republic* sank in 1908, the captain told passengers as they came to the lifeboats, "Remember! Women and children go first, then the First Cabin, then the others!"

class system operating in society at the time—a system which was very unfair. What do you think? Can the system itself be considered a villain?

Green heroes

Greenpeace is an organisation made up of ordinary people dedicated to protecting our planet's environment. To many people, Greenpeace actions are heroic. But those organisations and people whose actions are hindered or stopped by protests see Greenpeace and its activists as villains.

Over the years Greenpeace has strongly protested the testing of nuclear weapons, which can have devastating effects on the environment.

In 1985, the Greenpeace vessel, *Rainbow Warrior*, was docked at Auckland Harbour in New Zealand. The crew were making preparations for a protest voyage to the French nuclear test site at Moruroa Atoll. On the night of 10 July, a bomb exploded on board the *Rainbow Warrior*, sinking the vessel. A member of the crew, photographer Fernando Pereira, was killed by the blast.

When nuclear bombs are exploded under the sea, there is no cloud to be seen. But that doesn't mean there is no damage to the environment.

At first, France denied any involvement in the incident. But, it was later discovered that French secret service agents were responsible for the bombing. New Zealand Prime Minister, David Lange, described the incident as "Nothing more than a sordid act of international state-backed terrorism".

The name, *Rainbow Warrior*, was inspired by a Native American legend which says that after people have destroyed the world through greed, the Warriors of the Rainbow will arise to save it again.

The following year, France apologised and made a compensation payment of $NZ13 million ($US6.5 million) in return for the release into French custody of the two secret service agents who were held by New Zealand police.

Many people around the world saw the French government as villains, and the *Rainbow Warrior* crew as heroes. But to the French government, who regarded their nuclear tests as totally legal and within their rights, the *Rainbow Warrior* crew were the villains who had to be disabled.

Could you be a hero?

Extraordinary circumstances can turn ordinary people into heroes or villains.

There were reports of passengers and crew aboard the *Titanic* selflessly helping others, and reports of those who were only interested in saving themselves. What would you have done if you were aboard the *Titanic*?

There are often stories about ordinary people who have done extraordinary things, putting themselves at risk to help other people—saving people from drowning, helping to put out fires, coming to the assistance of someone in trouble. They are all ordinary people, but they are also heroes.

Every day, there are ordinary people who will take a stand, who will conquer their fears, who will not give up. Every day, there are ordinary people being heroic.

Could you be a hero?

Where to from here?

If you would like to know more about heroes and villains, a good place to start is your school library. There are lots of books covering the historical events and the people you have just read about.

The Internet is also a good resource. A starting point is StudyWeb:

http://www.studyweb.com

You can do a search on the person or event you're particularly interested in.

There are also numerous online encyclopaedia with information about mythology, folklore and legends that you can access:

http://www.pantheon.org/mythica/

http://www.optonline.com/content/ Learning/cmpt/Encyclopedia/

http://www.biography.com

If you would like to read a good story about an ordinary person who becomes a hero, then check out the companion Phenomena book, *Ordinary Hero*.

George's note

By doing research for this book I got the chance to learn about a lot of things—not just heroes and villains, although I did learn a lot about them too. I learnt about the American and French Revolutions, and the American and English Civil Wars. I learnt about the *Titanic* and the *Rainbow Warrior*. I learnt about the struggle for equal rights and about the spiritual beliefs of ancient civilisations.

I hope that by reading this book, you develop an interest in all these things too. "Heroes and Villains" is a very broad topic—a topic that can lead you to discover a whole range of other things because you will find heroes and villains in most historical events. There are lots more books in the Phenomena series, and although they all cover different topics, there are heroes or villains in all of them.

So, now that you've finished reading this book, go out and discover all those other topics.

Index